DATE DUE	DATE DUE	DATE DUE
17. 95	12. DEC 83	
5/10/93		
25 JAN 94		
12 feb 94		
26. FEB 94		
04. JUL 94		

GOING HOME TO RUSSIA

Paul Durcan

THE
BLACKSTAFF
PRESS
BELFAST AND WOLFEBORO, NEW HAMPSHIRE

ACKNOWLEDGEMENTS

The *Antigonish Review* (Nova Scotia); *Cyphers*; *Fortnight*; *Gown*; the *Irish Press* (New Irish Writing); the *Irish Times*; the *Irish Review*; *An Múinteoir*; *Rant*; *Rostrum*; RTE Radio One (*The Poet's Voice*); *Stand*; The Project Arts Centre and Taylor Galleries

First published in 1987 by
The Blackstaff Press Limited
3 Galway Park, Dundonald, Belfast BT16 0AN, Northern Ireland
and
27 South Main Street, Wolfeboro, New Hampshire 03894 USA
with the assistance of
The Arts Council of Northern Ireland

Typeset by The Brown Fox
Printed by Biddles Limited

British Library Cataloguing in Publication Data
Durcan, Paul
Going home to Russia.
I. Title
821'.914   PR6054.U47/

Library of Congress Cataloging-in-Publication Data
Durcan, Paul, 1944—
Going home to Russia.
I. Title.
PR6054.U72G65   1987   821'.914   87-18576
ISBN   0-85640-386-5

Dear M, this is for you

I have not intended to lead anyone anywhere, for the poet is simply a tree, which rustles on and on, but does not propose to lead anyone anywhere.

– B. L. Pasternak

Either everything will be possible, or everything will be absolutely impossible.

– V. Rasputin

But we, who've been born in an alien land,
With our fate of wandering and pride –
Should we seek to borrow a native land?

– I. Ratushinskaya

CONTENTS

Part I

Part II

PART
I

Six Nuns Die in Convent Inferno

To the
happy memory of six Loreto nuns
who died
between midnight and morning of
2 June 1986

I

We resided in a Loreto convent in the centre of Dublin city
On the east side of a public gardens, St Stephen's Green.
Grafton Street – the *paseo*
Where everybody *paseo'd*, including even ourselves –
Debouched on the north side, and at the top of Grafton Street,
Or round the base of the great patriotic pebble of O'Donovan
   Rossa,
Knelt tableaus of punk girls and punk boys.
When I used pass them – scurrying as I went –
Often as not to catch a Mass in Clarendon Street,
The Carmelite church in Clarendon Street
(Myself, I never used the Clarendon Street entrance,
I always slipped in by way of Johnson's Court,
Opposite the side entrance to Bewley's Oriental Café)
I could not help but smile, as I sucked on a Fox's mint,
That for all the half-shaven heads and the martial garb
And the dyed hair-dos and the nappy pins
They looked so conventional, really, and vulnerable,
Clinging to warpaint and to uniforms and to one another.
I knew it was myself who was the ultimate drop-out,
The delinquent, the recidivist, the vagabond,
The wild woman, the subversive, the original punk.
Yet, although I confess I was smiling, I was also afraid,
Appalled by my own nerve, my own fervour,
My apocalyptic enthusiasm, my other-worldly hubris:
To opt out of the world and to

Choose such exotic loneliness,
Such terrestrial abandonment,
A lifetime of bicycle lamps and bicycle pumps,
A lifetime of galoshes stowed under the stairs,
A lifetime of umbrellas drying out in the kitchen.

I was an old nun – an agèd beadswoman –
But I was no daw.
I knew what a weird bird I was, I knew that when we
Went to bed we were as eerie an aviary as you'd find
In all the blown-off rooftops of the city:
Scuttling about our dorm, wheezing, shrieking, croaking,
In our yellowy corsets, wonky suspenders, strung-out garters,
A bony crew in the gods of the sleeping city.
Many's the night I lay awake in bed
Dreaming what would befall us if there were a fire:
No fire-escapes outside, no fire-extinguishers inside;
To coin a Dublin saying,
We'd not stand a snowball's chance in hell. Fancy that!
It seemed too good to be true:
Happy death vouchsafed only to the few.
Sleeping up there was like sleeping at the top of the mast
Of a nineteenth century schooner, and in the daytime
We old nuns were the ones who crawled out on the yardarms
To stitch and sew the rigging and the canvas.
To be sure we were weird birds, oddballs, Christniks,
For we had done the weirdest thing a woman can do –
Surrendered the marvellous passions of girlhood,
The innocent dreams of childhood,
Not for a night or a weekend or even a Lent or a season,
But for a lifetime.
Never to know the love of a man or a woman;
Never to have children of our own;
Never to have a home of our own;
All for why and for what?
To follow a young man – would you believe it –

Who lived two thousand years ago in Palestine
And who died a common criminal strung up on a tree.

As we stood there in the disintegrating dormitory
Burning to death in the arms of Christ –
O Christ, Christ, come quickly, quickly –
Fluttering about in our tight, gold bodices,
Beating our wings in vain,
It reminded me of the snaps one of the sisters took
When we took a seaside holiday in 1956
(The year Cardinal Mindszenty went into hiding
In the US legation in Budapest.
He was a great hero of ours, Cardinal Mindszenty,
Any of us would have given our right arm
To have been his nun – darning his socks, cooking his meals,
Making his bed, doing his washing and ironing).
Somebody – an affluent buddy of the bishop's repenting his
    affluence –
Loaned Mother Superior a secluded beach in Co.
    Waterford –
Ardmore, along the coast from Tramore –
A cove with palm trees, no less, well off the main road.
There we were, fluttering up and down the beach,
Scampering hither and thither in our starched
    bathing-costumes.
Tonight, expiring in the fire, was quite much like that,
Only instead of scampering into the waves of the sea,
Now we were scampering into the flames of the fire.

That was one of the gayest days of my life,
The day the sisters went swimming.
Often in the silent darkness of the chapel after Benediction,
During the Exposition of the Blessed Sacrament,
I glimpsed the sea again as it was that day.
Praying – daydreaming really –
I became aware that Christ is the ocean

Forever rising and falling on the world's shore.
Now tonight in the convent Christ is the fire in whose waves
We are doomed but delighted to drown.
And, darting in and out of the flames of the dormitory,
Gabriel with that extraordinary message of his on his boyish
    lips,
Frenetically pedalling his skybike.
He whispers into my ear what I must do
And I do it – and die.
Each of us in our own tiny, frail, furtive way
Was a Mother of God, mothering forth illegitimate Christs
In the street life of Dublin city.
God have mercy on our whirring souls –
Wild women were we all –
And on the misfortunate, poor fire-brigade men
Whose task it will be to shovel up our ashes and shovel
What is left of us into black plastic refuse sacks.
Fire-brigade men are the salt of the earth.

Isn't it a marvellous thing how your hour comes
When you least expect it? When you lose a thing,
Not to know about it until it actually happens?
How, in so many ways, losing things is such a refreshing
    experience,
Giving you a sense of freedom you've not often experienced?
How lucky I was to lose – I say, lose – lose my life.
It was a Sunday night, and after Vespers
I skipped Bathroom so that I could hop straight into bed
And get in a bit of a read before Lights Out:
Conor Cruise O'Brien's new book *The Siege*,
All about Israel and superlatively insightful
For a man who they say is reputedly an agnostic –
I got a loan of it from the brother-in-law's married niece –
But I was tired out and I fell asleep with the book open
Face down across my breast and I woke
To the racket of bellowing flame and snarling glass.

The first thing I thought was that the brother-in-law's
    married niece
Would never again get her Conor Cruise O'Brien back
And I had seen on the price-tag that it cost £23.00:
Small wonder that the custom of snipping off the price
As an exercise in social deportment has simply died out;
Indeed a book today is almost worth buying for its price,
Its price frequently being more remarkable than its contents.

The strange Eucharist of my death –
To be eaten alive by fire and smoke.
I clasped the dragon to my breast
And stroked his red-hot ears.
Strange! There we were, all sleeping molecules,
Suddenly all giving birth to our deaths,
All frantically in labour.
Doctors and midwives weaved in and out
In gowns of smoke and gloves of fire.
Christ, like an Orthodox patriarch in his dressing-gown,
Flew up and down the dormitory, splashing water on our
    souls:
Sister Eucharia; Sister Seraphia; Sister Rosario;
Sister Gonzaga; Sister Margaret; Sister Edith.
If you will remember us – six nuns burnt to death –
Remember us for the frisky girls that we were,
Now more than ever – kittens in the sun.

II

When Jesus heard these words at the top of Grafton Street
Uttered by a small, agèd, emaciated, female punk
Clad all in mourning black, and grieving like an alley cat,
He was annulled with astonishment, and turning round
He declared to the gangs of teenagers and dicemen following
    him:

'I tell you, not even in New York city
Have I found faith like this.'

That night in St Stephen's Green,
After the keepers had locked the gates,
And the courting couples had found cinemas themselves to
    die in,
The six nuns who had died in the convent inferno,
From the bandstand they'd been hiding under, crept out
And knelt together by the Fountain of the Three Fates,
Reciting the Agnus Dei: reciting it as if it were the torch song
Of all aid – Live Aid, Self Aid, AIDS, and All Aid –
Lord, I am not worthy
That thou should'st enter under my roof;
Say but the word and my soul shall be healed.

PART
II

The Rape of Europa

(after Titian)

to Seamus and Marie

'Is life a dream' – my sleeping daughter beseeches me,
Gaping up at me anxiously out of the ashes of her sleep
As I bend down low over her to kiss her goodnight –
'I was playing on the shore with the other girls,
Under the cliff where the Car Assembly Works is,
When the man who works in Mr Conway's field,
The big fellow who lives alone and who always says hallo,
Casually came striding towards us through the barbed wire,
The muscles in his arms rippling in the sun
As if the empty sandhills were packed stadiums,
And his body – he had left off all his clothes –
Was a nude of crimson triangles of blood,
Where the barbs had pierced his snow-white flesh;
The other girls began to cry –
I do not know why I did not also begin to cry,
Only I thought he looked quite beautiful the way he was.
The more I gazed into his grassy eyes
The more his wounds from the barbed wire appeared to teem
Until curly hair sprouted from each wound, and big floppy
    ears,
And his mouth and nostrils became one large wet slithery
    snout,
And when he leaned over towards me, putting his two hands
On the yellow sand, they changed into hooves,
And two legs fell down slowly out of his backside
With a thin, smiling tail the length of a clothesline.
He curled up on the sand and he looked so forlorn
I thought of how I would like to go to sleep on his back
And caress his hide with my hand round his horn
And pillow my face in his shoulderblades

11

And float off across the ocean to the Island of Bulls
In whose blue and red skies
I could see astronaut babies cascading in embryos.
And when I asked him if he would give me a ride
He lowed as if the dusk was a towel on his brow
And I put flowers on his head,
Flowers which I had been gathering with the other girls
In the seaside meadows among the hills of fern –
Wild rose, yellow crocus, narcissus, violet, hyacinth –
And just then as I mounted him you came into my bedroom
And I looked up and I saw you
Bending low over me to kiss me goodnight.
Life is a dream, Papa, isn't it? Life is a dream?'

'Life is a dream, Phoenix, life is a dream.
Go back to sleep now and have a wild ride on your bull
For there's only noise to lose when quietude is on the
    rampage.
Dream is life's element and symbol – as the sea's the eel's;
We expire if we're deprived of our element and symbol.
Smeared, daubed, licked, bloodied in entrails of dream.
If the bull has loosed the paddock of his flesh it means
That boys might once more again be boys and girls girls –
Not entrepreneurs and shareholders in the Car Assembly
    Works,
To be assessed and calculated in the files of newspapers.
When you wake up in the morning –
Before you brush your teeth, before even you say your
    prayers –
Turn over on your back and count
The big fellow who works in Mr Conway's field
As you count sheep when you're going to sleep;
Count all the babies who have never been born
As well as all the babies who have been born.
If you're late for school, I'll write a note for teacher.
Sleep, Phoenix, sleep.'

The Late Mr Charles Lynch Digresses

to Síabhra

Having sat all morning at the bay window
Of the run-down boarding house on the bitch-bedecked hill
Overlooking the drowned city of Cork
With a long-stemmed wine-glass balancing on the fulcrum
Of his ladylike, crossed knees – the deceased virtuoso
In the threadbare black greatcoat and frayed white shirt
Tiptoes through the urban heat
And scrupulously digresses into the Cork School of Music
When, from next door's crucial radio studios,
A production technician, Evie, comes skittering –
'Mr Lynch, they necessitate you urgently next door.'
Without altering the adagio of his gait, or its cantabile,
The ghostly pianist, the master digresser,
Perilously whispers:
'I'm sorry, Evie – but I'm *dashing*.'

Nora Dreaming of Kilcash

All in all, I have had a lucky life.
What mishaps have befallen me
I have endured.
Such as when chasing after the boy next door
And I ran through his plate-glass door
I had to have my two hands amputated
– *Dechirée* –
As in the French the language so delicately has it.
My primary difficulty has remained in the area of love.
Such men as have fallen in love with me
Have gone only so far and no farther –
To the cinema, to the seaside, to the woods.
Whenever I mention 'living together'
They fall silent, or smile, or change the subject.
When once I said to Kilcash 'Is it my hands?'
He replied 'Yes, it's your hands' – and he drove off.
I look down at my hands – my hands that I haven't got –
And I smile at my feet, my dainty, faithful feet.
Certainly I am lonely – lonelier than you will ever know.
But I've got feet, I can tell you, I've got feet.
When I die I'll leave my shoes behind me
On the floorboards by the wainscoting in a row,
All nine pairs of them, all spic and dust-bejewelled,
High heels grazing by the edge of the Western Ocean.
I've got feet, I can tell you, I've got feet.

EI Flight 106: New York–Dublin

(after J.M.W. Turner)

There was an empty seat between us as the jumbo began to
    taxi
And she – a craggy girl of about seventy-five years of age –
Leaned over and whispered conspiratorially, huskily:
'We've got an empty seat to ourselves – between ourselves.'
She winked, all her wing-flaps trembling,
Slashes of eyeshadow, daubs of rouge,
Her eyes roving around in their sockets as they scoured me
For what pusillanimous portions of manhood I might
    possess.
She exuded femininity as an elephant exudes hide:
Wearing all of her seventy-five years as ethereally
As an adolescent girl wearing earrings.
'We've got an empty seat to ourselves,' she rasped
As I gazed at her pink, silk, sleeveless dress with turquoise
    triskeles
And at her moist, fiery eyes rearing up in her skull.
'Ladies and gentlemen, our feature film tonight is *The
    Flamingo Kid*.
We'll be commencing our take-off in approximately five
    minutes.'
As we continued to taxi she showed me her bottle of
    drambuie –
'Duty-free!'
High over Kennedy, as we turned tail on Manhattan,
Heading out over Long Island for the North Atlantic,
She had a member of the cabin crew fetch her a baby scotch
And a tumbler choc-a-bloc with ice-cubes.
'I don't drink myself,' she sighed tremulously
As I stared helplessly down at the Cape Cod coastline,
'Except of course when I'm flying.
Rusty Nails is what I like – Drambuie and scotch.'

15

I could not keep my eyes off her as she guzzled it down,
And the urban necklaces far below on the breast of the
    coastline.
'Do you know,' she remarked, 'you are a truly handsome little
    man.
I feel proud to be sitting beside you – with an empty seat
    between us.'
Before I could begin to make my puny reply, she added:
'Cheer up – the worst that could happen would be if we
    crashed.
Imagine floating about in the midst of all this debris and
    wreckage.'
I glanced around at my 350 fellow passengers,
All sunset and chains.
She disembarked at Shannon at dawn in the mist
And I flew on to Dublin, not worried whether I lived to tell
    the tale
Of how I had had the great good fortune
To fly from New York to Dublin with *The Flamingo Kid*
Clutching a glass of Rusty Nails in her freckled claws,
Her beaked eyes playing on the floodwaters of her smile:
'Cheer up – the worst that could happen would be if we
    crashed.
Imagine floating about in the midst of all this debris and
    wreckage.'

Cardinal Dies of Heart Attack in Dublin Brothel

Edifying, edifying – you cry – edifying –
As in silence we sit listening to the six o'clock tv news
That our belovèd cardinal has died
In the arms of his favourite prostitute.
At last – I think to myself in the solitude of my soul –
A sign that the church of God is moving into the light.

I put on my overcoat and, as there are rainclouds,
I take the precaution of bringing along my umbrella.
I have to walk the long way round to the church
Whose candlelit darkness proves always consoling.
I insert a 50p piece in the moneybox and light three candles:
One for the Cardinal, one for the Lady,
And one for the Unknown Soldier in all of us.
I kneel down in a pew to pray
But I quickly translate myself into a sitting position.
The sitting position is my natural position.
My soul is borne up on wings of flame
In which I think again of the agèd cardinal's submission
To that lovely, ephemeral woman
And of her compassion which, by all accounts,
Was as tender as it was fiery.
I depart the church, feeling restored in body and soul.
As you say, my dear wife, with your characteristic wit
And solicitude – our belovèd cardinal who has died in a
    brothel
Was, in the very last analysis, 'a broth of a cardinal'.

Irish Church Comes in From the Cold

It was on an Air Canada flight from London to Montreal
That I learned, quite by chance, from a Redemptorist priest
Who was sitting in a non-smoking seat across the aisle
    from me
Of the good news that in a chapel in Limerick
There had been installed a rack of contraceptives –
In a profane world I could feel the heartbeat of the sacred.

'Candles: Ten Pence Each' – it is written – and I insert
A tenpenny coin into the lip of the moneybox
And I light a candle off another candle
And I plant it in the top rung thinking of the woman I love
And likewise I insert a second coin in the adjacent rack
And piously put in my pocket a packet of condoms.
I return to my pew and sit there praying and daydreaming.
I find sitting, rather than kneeling,
More conducive to praying and daydreaming.
I pray to St John of the Cross and to all the great lovers
And to all the women of the world who have had rhyme and
    reason,
As well as good cause, to love and to cherish their men.

Priest Accused of Not Wearing Condom

A forty-two-year-old parish priest – Fr Francey Mulholland –
Was charged yesterday in the Circuit Criminal Court
With not wearing a condom, and with intent
To cause an unwanted pregnancy.
Fr Mulholland pleaded guilty to both charges.
Pleading for leniency, counsel for Fr Mulholland
Stated that the priest was ignorant in the use of condoms,
Coming as he did from a farming background,
And that if he had known how to operate a condom
He would most certainly have operated a condom.
Sentencing the accused to two years' hard labour
Judge Gemma FitzGerald stated that it was disturbing
In this day and age, and in this progressive country,
That a priest should contemplate not wearing a condom
And when it was a case of a young, virile, parish priest
Like Fr Mulholland, it was doubly disturbing
And not only doubly disturbing but singularly scandalous.
She recommended that while serving his sentence
Fr Mulholland should be given access to condom therapy.
Perhaps – she commented – he is lacking in condom
    consciousness.
Leave to appeal was granted, as was bail
On condition that Fr Mulholland satisfied the Gardaí
That he was in full possession of, and at all times,
The Joy of Sex by Dr Alex Comfort,
The devotional sex manual recently banned by the State
    Censorship.
Judge Gemma added that it was gallant of the bailswoman,
Fr Mulholland's girlfriend, to go bail for the priest,
Considering the gravity of the offence to her person.
The bailswoman, Ms Liz Graves, stated that Fr Mulholland
Had promised her never again not to wear a condom.
The couple left the courtroom
To the rousing applause of their families and their friends,

Not to mention three or four stalwart bishops cheering meekly in the distant background.

The Leader and the Leader Writer

When Giles Moroney wrote his leader about the leader
At five o'clock in the afternoon over a cup of black coffee
Little did he know that he would be spending that night
In bed with his leader.
Life is full of surprises:
From Coolock to Tulsa,
From Samarkand to Mulhuddart.
As they lay together, awake in bed,
The leader writer and the leader,
In the watches of the night
Lit up by the luminous green numerals
Of the digital bedside clock radio
(A gift to the leader from another leader –
The Emperor of the Mountmellick Urban District Council)
The leader writer apprised the leader
That he had written a leader about the leader
For tomorrow's newspaper.
The leader conjectured what the leader writer
Had written about him in tomorrow's newspaper.

Another morning – another darkness – another day.
The leader looked at himself in the looking-glass,
Wondering what the leader writer had written about him:
'When our leader looks at himself in the looking-glass,
Is it himself he sees or is it somebody else?
Or can it be that he is looking in the wrong mirror?
We feel it is our duty to point out to the leader
That it is time that he purchased a new mirror:
A leader must be master in his own bedroom.'
Putting aside the newspaper the leader yawned
And put his arm around the curly head of the leader writer:
'I like you enormously but you're a cheeky leader writer.
What I need is not a new mirror but a new hair style.'
The cocky young leader writer sat up in the bed:

21

'Leader, I love you for your hairstyle and not yourself alone.
If you dare to alter it, I will write a vituperative leader
And I promise you, I promise you, I will never again share
   with you
A bunch of pillows, or the sonorities of the double bed.'
But the leader smiled, tickling and punching
His leader writer in the solar plexus:
'There, there, there now, my darling leader writer,
If you're a good boy – but a very good boy –
Your leader will write your next leader for you.'
The leader writer lay back down again in the bed with a
   groan:
It's the double beds, not the corridors, of power that count.

What Shall I Wear, Darling, to *The Great Hunger*?

What shall I wear, darling, to *The Great Hunger*?
She shrieked at me helplessly from the east bedroom
Where the west wind does be blowing betimes.
I did not hesitate to hazard a spontaneous response:
'Your green evening gown –
Your see-through, sleeveless, backless, green evening gown.'
We arrived at the Peacock
In good time for everybody to have a good gawk at her
Before the curtain went up on *The Great Hunger*.
At the interval everybody was clucking about, cooing
That it was simply stunning – her dress –
'Darling, you look like Mother Divinity in your see-through,
Sleeveless, backless, green evening gown – it's so visual!'
At the party after the show – simply everyody was there –
Winston Lenihan, Consolata O'Carroll-Riviera, Yves
    St Kirkegaard –
She was so busy being admired that she forgot to get drunk.
But the next morning it was business as usual –
Grey serge pants, blue donkey jacket – driving around
    Dolphin's Barn
In her Opel Kadett hatchback
Checking up on the rents. 'All these unmarried young
    mothers
And their frogspawn, living on the welfare –
You would think that it never occurs to them
That it's their rents that pay for the outfits I have to wear
Whenever *The Great Hunger* is playing at the Peacock.
No, it never occurs to them that in Ireland Today
It is not easy to be a landlord and a patron of the arts.
It is not for nothing that we in Fail Gael have a social
    conscience:
Either you pay the shagging rent or you get out on the street.
Next week I have to attend three-and-a-half *Great Hunger*s,
Not to mention a half-dozen *Juno and the Paycock*s.'

Lisa, Don't Sell Robbed Gear to the Grahams

That you're my daughter, Lisa, and I'm your father
Does not seem to matter a curse to you
Except when you want a John McCormack off me;
But, on my bended knees, I beg of you,
Lisa, don't sell robbed gear to the Grahams.
Last evening in the tunnel under the railway bridge
By the Dodder River when I emerged out of the dark
And I saw you loitering there and you jeered at me
And you told me to take a running jump for myself –
'You're only my father – will you leave me alone!' –
I wanted to put my arms around you and hold you tight
And to take you away on a holiday and never come back.
I loved you from the day you were born and I love you
    tonight,
Lisa – don't sell robbed gear to the Grahams.

The Poetry Reading Last Night in the Royal Hibernian Hotel

The main thing – the first and last thing – to say
About the poetry reading last night in the Royal Hibernian
    Hotel
Is that the Royal Hibernian Hotel does not exist;
It was demolished last year to make way for an office block.
If, therefore, anyone was to ask me what a poetry reading is,
I should have the utmost difficulty in enlightening them,
All the more so after having attended last night's poetry
    reading
In the Royal Hibernian Hotel which does not exist.
A poetry reading appears to be a type of esoteric social ritual
Peculiar to the cities of northern Europe and North America.
What happens is that for one reason or another,
Connected usually with moods in adolescence
To do with Family and School and Sexuality,
A chap – or a dame – begins writing things
Which he – she – calls 'Poetry'
And over the years – especially between the ages of fourteen
    and sixty-four –
What with one kind of wangling or another,
He – she – publishes seventeen or nineteen slim volumes
Entitled *Stones* or *Bricks* or *Pebbles* or *Gravel*;
Or *History Notes* or *Digs* or *French Class*.
He – she – is hellbent on boring the pants off people
And that's where the poetry-reading trick comes in.
The best poets are the poets who can bore you the most,
Such as the fellow last night who was so adept at boring us
That for the entire hour that he stood there mumbling and
    whining
My mind was altogether elsewhere with the reindeer
In Auden's Cemetery for the Silently and Very Fast.
A poetry reading is a ritual in communal schizophrenia
In which the minds of the audience are altogether elsewhere
While their bodies are kept sitting upright or in position.

Afterwards it is the custom to clap as feebly as you can –
A subtle exercise appropriate to the overall scheme.
To clap feebly – or to feebly clap – is as tricky as it sounds.
It is the custom then to invite the poet to autograph the slim
    volume
And while the queue forms like the queue outside a
    confessional,
The poet cringing archly on an upright chair,
You say to your neighbour 'A fine reading, wasn't it?'
To which he must riposte
'Indeed – nice to see you lying through your teeth.'
The fully clothèd audience departs, leaving the poet
Who bored the pants off them
Laughing all the way to the toilet
Of a hotel that does not exist,
Thence to the carpark that *does* exist
Where he has left his Peugeot with the broken exhaust pipe.
'Night-night' – he mews to the automatic carpark attendant
Who replies with one bright, emphatic, onomatopoeic
    monosyllable:
'Creep.'

The Divorce Referendum, Ireland, 1986

By the time the priest started into his sermon
I was adrift on a leaf of tranquillity,
Feeling only the need and desire to praise,
To feed praise to the tiger of life.
Hosanna, Hosanna, Hosanna.
He was a gentle-voiced, middle-aged man,
Slightly stooped under a gulf of grey hair,
Slightly tormented by an excess of humility.
He talked felicitously of the Holy Spirit –
As if he really believed in what he was preaching –
Not as if he was aiming to annotate a diagram
Or to sub-edit the gospel,
But as if the Holy Spirit was real as rainwater.
Then his voice changed colour –
You could see it change from pink into white.
He remarked icily: 'It is the wish of the Hierarchy
That today the clergy of Ireland put before you
Christ's teaching on the indissolubility of marriage
And to remind you that when you vote in the Divorce
    Referendum
The Church's teaching and Christ's teaching are one and the
    same.'
Stunned, I stared up at him from my pew
As he stood there supported by candles and gladioli,
Vestments, and altarboys at his feet;
I could feel my breastplate tighten and my shoulderblades
    quiver;
I knew the anger that Jesus Christ felt
When he drove from the temple the traders and stockbrokers.
I have come into this temple today to pray
And be healed by, and joined with, the Spirit of Life;
Not to be invaded by ideology.
I say unto you, preacher, and orators of the Hierarchy,
Do not bring ideology into my house of prayer.

I closed my eyes
And I did not open them again until I could hear
The priest murmuring the prayers of the Consecration.
At Holy Communion I kept my eyes on a small girl
To whom the priest had to bend low to give her the host.
Curtseying, she smiled eagerly, and flew back down the aisle,
Carrying in her breast the Eucharist of her innocence:
May she have children of her own
And as many husbands as will praise her –
For what are husbands for, but to praise their wives?

The Anglo-Irish Agreement, 1986

to Constance Short

I

The British Army barracks in Crossmaglen
Has the air of an exclusive suburb in Dublin:
All silent and inimical, aloof and airy.
Except for the toings and froings of helicopters and crickets
You could hear a pin drop – or a bomb.
Strolling across the village square in Crossmaglen
You might be in Ailesbury Road in Ballsbridge
Where each detached and fortress-visaged residence
Has the air of a habitat inhabited by no one.
There are two hundred troops inside the British Army
    barracks
But you would never know it – no more than you would
    know
That there is a solicitor on £130,000 a year
Inside that mansion with his wife and two children.
All armies
Are armies of occupation.
The exclusive suburbs of Dublin city
Are necklaces of Crossmaglens
In which armies of occupation fester
Behind fortified walls and electronically controlled gates.

II

Let the armies exchange uniforms.
Let the British Army in Crossmaglen
Patrol the village square in Nissan Bluebirds
Or in chauffeur-driven Datsun Laurels
And wear Celtic pinstripe suits on duty
Or Laura Ashley frocks,

While in Ailesbury Road and Clyde Road,
Elgin, Raglan and Shrewsbury,
Let the residents disport
In British Army uniform,
Mothers-in-law and newly marrieds
Darting in and out of gateways with bayonets at the ready,
Walkie-talkies and back-packs.
The Anglo-Irish Agreement
Which has been in force
For longer than we can remember –
For at least sixty-four years and more likely
Eleven thousand years –
Should make it mandatory for residents of Ballsbridge
– Killiney and Rathgar, Foxrock and Howth –
To do a tour of duty
In the British Army barracks in Crossmaglen.
The rest of us can pretend to be natives –
What we have always been,
Working-class people in our place.

The House Where There are No Women

to Richard, Anne and Simone

I wrap the white towel – bloody – around my face.
It is time to stand up.

In the house where there are no women,
That house is empty;
Its emptiness fills not only itself,
It fills all the hillside.

We are speaking of the tallest hillside in Ireland;
It tilts – in a gale it stands fast.
It is the house where there are no women.
Did it fall? It fell.

It fell – the daughters slain, a pair.
Their souls are wild flowers.
Their eyes are mushrooms in autumn.
I am their father. I know.

How does it begin? How does it end?
Thomas Hardy asked.
Not with life, and, most certainly, not with death.

We love. We
Die.

Family Planning Clinic, Easter Sunday Morning

My telephone number is 604471
But I keep getting calls for 604417
Which is the number
Of the Family Planning Clinic.
On Easter Sunday morning
(It had been a week since the last
Telephone call; it had been
A week since I had last
Had verbal, or any other kind
Of contact with a member of the species)
The telephone detonated into life
And I barged out of bed and lunged
Down the creaking stairs
In my faded pink dressing gown
– And matching frayed pink slippers –
Picked up the receiver and listened to the soft
Caring voice of a young woman – O –
And she whispered: 'Hallo, is that' –
And she paused – and I waited for her to say 'Paul
Durcan' but she did not say anything
And I said: 'I beg your pardon' –
And she said: 'Who is that?'
As if she were a trifle perplexed, a trifle fearful,
And I said: 'This is Paul Durcan' –
And she said: 'I'm sorry – Wrong Number.'
And she put down the phone.

Dejected, I trickled back up the creaking stairs to bed
– Headlong once more, but not very –
And assiduously inserting myself between the sheets,
Assiduously pigeonholing my skull in the pillows,
I gazed round at my four white walls, savouring
The first fruits of yet another Easter Sunday.
It's a nice enough name, I think to myself – Wrong Number –

Preferable at any rate to the name I have got:
Paul Durcan – what an appalling appellation.
I wish there were more Family Planning Clinics in Ireland.
How orchestral, not to say metamorphic,
To have been christened Wrong Number.
'Good morning, Mr Number! How is it going, Wrong?'

A Swipe at a Four-Leggèd, Long-Tailed Stammer

For two years I went out with Alva Davidson
But in the end, not surprisingly, she threw me up.
What particularly irked her was when we'd bump
Into casual acquaintances of mine and I'd always fail
To introduce her to them – naturally she interpreted it
As a form of rejection, neglect, wilful indifference.
The truth, however, lay fallow in another lie:
For two years I had managed to conceal from her
The existence and whereabouts of my stammer;
Yet her surname presented me with insuperable difficulties
Because it began with the letter D.
The letter D was a fence too steep for my stammer
And that was why I could not introduce her to strangers.
I could say, with a flourish, 'This is Alva – '
But I could not follow it up with 'Davidson'.
At best I could manage 'Day . . .'
The last time it happened was on the staircase of the Gaiety
    Theatre
When who should buttonhole me but Peter Christie.
'Hallo Peter – this is Alva Day . . .'
I simply could not sustain it and, besides,
The lid of my diaphragm was about to blow off.
The three of us smiled and curtseyed and blushed and
    barked:
'Ach, yes'; 'oh, well'; 'so'.

In the weeks before Alva finally gave me the heave-ho
I toyed with the idea of discussing my stammer with her –
Of *sharing* my stammer with her, as the therapists would
    put it.
But she was not keen on mice, and my stammer
Is a species of house mouse which inhabits
The cubbyholes immediately beneath my cheekbones.
If I squeeze my two cheekbones with my forefingers

I can immediately hear my stammer squealing –
Which is why it prefers to creep down my larynx
And lurk in the doorway of my cardiac household.
If you have been adhering prayerfully to these words
   of my pain
You will have heard a gnawing sound between their syllables:
The mouse of my stammer gnawing at the door of my heart.
O God of everything-that-went-wrong-in-my-childhood-and-
   all-the-rest-of-my-adolescence-and-youth
Please let me introduce you to Alva Davidson.

The Kalahari, Pimlico, and the West of Ireland

I

Boy and Girl back to back, rubbing backsides:
A ritual of courtship, not to be mocked at.
It is the same in the West of Ireland as in the Kalahari
And Pimlico –
On dark summer's evenings in meadows and courtyards
Boys and Girls stalk one another, yearning
To avert their eyes, instead
To let their backsides speak for them;
To crouch down in the long grass, backside to backside –
No more virginal form of intimacy can be envisioned.
We, as teenagers, we know – only our parents
Have fallen under the thrall of prophets and auctioneers
And bartered our native way of life for bungalow bliss.
No greater trust can a woman have in a man
Than to bare her backside, and he his to her,
Backside to backside, for we trust in the Silence of God.

II

Of all the members and parts of my body
It is my backside of which I am most neglectful.
Yet it is my backside which serves me
More faithfully than any other part or member.
How many hours in the week do you spend
Complacently sprawling on your backside,
Freeloading on your backside
While your feet smirk in a pair of Italian shoes
And newspapers gloat in your hands?
How many years have you sat on your backside
Without so much as a syllable of gratitude?
Yet while all the rest of you disintegrates
From head to toe – teeth, chest, legs –

It is your reticent backside who never fails you.
Your backside which even when you are on your last legs
Will never let you down, will always say:
'I am here beneath you forever faithful and pliant.'
Why then am I ashamed of that part of me
Which is the most loyal and tender part,
Not to say the most bashful?
For I have never known a backside
That was not a wholesome and a pretty backside.
Why, even under a malevolent, switchback face
There lurks a pretty backside.
Even Ronald Reagan has a pretty backside.
Shame on shame that so betrays the backside.
Of all the human beings I have known
Only six or seven women had the courage of their backsides,
Women who without exception were noble spirits,
Chestnut-haired, soft-spoken, undaunted, cheeky.
But males are forever coy about their backsides,
Forever precious, as they are, about saving face.
You would never catch them saving backside.
When one of them has perpetrated a crime
His fellows put a price on his head,
Which shows yet again their neglect of basics,
Their ignorance of fundamentals;
Else, they'd put a price on his backside.
For it my backside that is my crowning glory
And, if only you knew that, you might respect me,
Instead of which you snigger and go to war
To beat my brains out on the plains of Hungary.

The Hay-Carrier

after Veronica Bolay

Have you ever saved hay in Mayo in the rain?
Have you ever made hay in Mayo in the sun?
Have you ever carried above your head a haycock
   on a pitchfork?
Have you ever slept in a haybarn on the road from
   Mayo into Egypt?
I am a hay-carrier.
My father was a hay-carrier.
My mother was a hay-carrier.
My brothers were hay-carriers.
My sisters were hay-carriers.
My wife is a hay-carrier.
My son is a hay-carrier.
His sons are hay-carriers.
His daughters are hay-carriers.
We were always all hay-carriers.
We will always be hay-carriers.
For the great gate of night stands painted red –
And all of heaven lies waiting to be fed.

A Vision of Africa on the Coast of Kerry

On the coast at Meenogahane,
Near Causeway,
Nellie presides in the kitchen of her cottage
At eighty-five, exchanging the time of day
With tourists, educating us:
Nellie who has never in her life
Been out of her townland
Except 'the wanst'.
Five years ago at eighty
When she had a stroke
She was transported
By county ambulance
To the Regional Hospital in Cork.
Do you know what I saw there?
No, Nellie, what did you see?
I saw a black man.
A black man?
A black man – you should have seen his neck!
His neck?
Oh the neck of him   the lovely neck of him –
The lovely, wet, shiny, rubbery neck of him!
I asked him if he would let me put my hand on it
And he did, he let me –
And it was all black, do you know?
Oh it was lovely, I tell you, lovely!

Dr Ronan Walsh and Surgeon Degas

Bats – that's what they say about me and my old lady.
A Pair of Bats – that's what they call us.
What they mean is that we're past it, and contemptible,
And scary to children,
An old man and his old wan living on the welfare
In two rooms of a condemned house at the back end of
    Clontarf.
Bats – what they mean is that we're ragged and poor,
The pair of us – loopy and spooky – two carrier bags of
    armpits.
And it's true that our habitat, if you want to call it that,
Is decrepit and dark – torn curtains, tin teapots, broken
    chairs –
And I don't have a bath every night of the week,
I don't have a bath every week,
In fact I don't have a bath at all.
There is no bath in the house where we live.
But if you really want to know us – maybe you don't –
I suggest you go down and see Dr Ronan W
(And he may or may not pass you on to Surgeon Degas)
And he'll show you X-rays of our lives –
The interior lives of a pair of old bats.
We're not past it. We're bats, alright, but we're not past it.
When we get into bed, the pair of us,
And snuggle up and writhe and hang upside down inside the
    sheets,
She in her tights and I in my vest,
All the coloured lights in the dark trees come alive
And we blow the fuses – every fucking fuse in the house – the
    children
Under our bedroom window playing house ever so delicately,
    solemnly,
While the trains overhead rumble home to the West of
    Ireland.

Shriek – be quiet. Be quiet – shriek.
That's that, my lovely old bat – bat;
That's that, my lovely old bat – bat.
When you analyse it, like Dr Ronan W,
You can see that she and me –
That we're quite a pair of trapeze artists, the pair of us,
Pipistrelles on bars – the city falling down all around us.

On Pleading Guilty to Being Heterosexual

Lunchtime, and I am crouched
In the corner of a Dublin pub,
Sipping at my packet soup,
Munching at my prepacked shepherd's pie,
When – miles above my loophole eyes –
A voice says to me
'Hallo there!'

There I am crouched in my glass ball,
Sealed in transparency,
All locked up inside my polythene membrane
Of ultraviolet individuality,
When – miles above my loophole eyes –
A voice says to me
'Hallo there!'

I look up and behold
The face of the barlady
Peering down at me,
All concupiscence and business,
As if her lips and eyes were one
– Or as if her eyes had teeth –
Her lips painted hot pink,
Her eyes agleam with mascara.
I can feel in one swoop
Her sexuality charge through me
And I light up like a tree
Leafing in the corner of the pub,
My face turning red to gold to green.

Now no one can ever say
That when a woman sensually,
Gratuitously, selflessly,
Showers coins down into the well

Of a lonely man's loneliness
She's not a woman and he's not a man.
To the charge of being heterosexual,
My Lord, I plead guilty:
Please sentence me to life –
And to a woman with teeth in her eyes.

Martha

I

My idea of heaven
Would be to live with a woman,
Not in a lovers' torment
But in friendship's contentment;
She's as good as she's bad
And she's the best friend I've never had.
I think she is beautiful:
She is as fierce as she is gentle
And she is neither less nor more
Than she ought to be. Pour
Her a story of freedom – give her
What she wants, and do not hurt her.
My idea of hell
Is when a woman says to me 'Farewell'.

II

Not to have married you was a great failure –

Which I salute but do not boast.
It is beside the point
That you would have refused
Point-blank to marry me –
Why, it could be said
You would rather have died
Than marry me.

Still, not to have married you was a great failure.

A small point,
But I think one worth mentioning,
Is my concept of marriage:

A noble friendship –
The noblest of all friendships –
In which the gifts of the mind
Are shared in the delights of the bed.

Not to have married you was a great failure.

If I could have wrested from you
Your huge impatience of me,
And put your head between my hands,
You could have put your tongue in my mouth
And drunk deep from my soul;
It would have pleased me
To have given myself to you.

Not to have married you was a great failure.

I smile when I think of you
Asleep in the countryside of the sea,
Bursting out all over in blackberries,
Wiping the mauve juice off your lips
With the sleeve of your jumper,
Your cunning quivering in sealight,
Moonmother composed of so many cupboards.

Not to have married you was a great failure.

Poem for Your Forty-Seventh Birthday

Wild Rose, forgive me if I do not presume to know
Who you are on your forty-seventh birthday:
Being in the prime of your life, as you are today,
Means being a woman to which only you are privy,
Your sisters, and your daughter;
A blur in purdah on a skyline in water;
Male sputniks such as I must sit outside the temple
Suspended in orbit, treading water in water.

As we encroach on the masked bloom of your forty-seventh
    incarnation
I lose sight of you and the mystery deepens,
Only to demist as the years ahead open up
And I contemplate the tall activist in her seventy-seventh
    year,
Caught in a moment of pedestalled stillness as she beholds
Under a blue wide-brimmed bonnet
The agèd face of her great-granddaughter
At her christening by a font of Dublin granite:

Two conjectural urchins
Who having long orbited on their silent, oblique trajectories
Today have come here together for a photo-call –
Close-up snap by the baptismal font, splashing.
Today is that baby's Minus Thirtieth Birthday –
Your Plus Forty-Seventh.
Who knows where you are now, where she is not?
Peace to her waters – to your clouds.

Martha's Wall

Her pleasure – what gave her pleasure – was to be walked
Down her wall, the South Wall, a skinny, crinkly, golden-
   stemmed wall
That contracts and expands, worms and unworms, in and
   out of Dublin Bay,
Across the sea's thighs pillowing in, besotted, under daisy-
   gartered skies.
She'd curl her finger around my finger and I'd lead her out
   on to it.
She liked it when the flowering sea was shedding spray
   across it.
She'd tense up with delight to see me get wet
And wetter still, and wetter – the wetter it was
The better she liked it, and me – and she wanted always
To get down, away down, to the very end of it
Where there is a deep-red lighthouse, and the deep-red
   lighthouse
Was hers also, hers, and we'd sit down on a bench under it
And she'd put her arm around my neck and we'd stop needing
   to speak
And we'd sit there, breathless, in silence, for a long time.

Girls Like Me Should Live a Thousand Years

I remember her as she was on her forty-eighth birthday.
She is a little tired – it has been a long day
At the office, and there have been many committee meetings
And press conferences, old files and new files,
Telegrams, memos, telexes, telephone calls.
She is a little tired, and she lies down on her couch –
Her red couch – face down, prone, on her red couch.
I kneel down on the floorboards beside her red couch
Holding her right hand, lightly holding her right hand.
I remember as she glanced up at me
  – Her utterly worldly-wise mouth, utterly guileless mouth –
Thinking that she had not changed since she was twelve
    years old,
And her big brown eyes did not blink as I grinned at her.
She stared at me:
Girls like me should live a thousand years.

The Orientalist

after Kitaj

The Ringsend Hermit.
The Ringsend Hermit?

And Orientalist.
And what?

The Orientalist.
The Orientalist.

And she's mad about him.
She's mad about him?

What's an Orientalist?
I haven't got an iota.

Men in women's clothes?
Men in women's clothes?

I think it's a . . .
Do you think it's a . . .

She'd know, I suppose.
Of course she'd know.

Do you think it means that he's a specialist in something?
He has the look of a specialist, right enough.

The fellow before him was a specialist as well, wasn't he?
*Yes, and the fellow before him also, and the fellow before him
    again.*

Yet not one of them had a home of his own.
On the other hand, she has a home of her own.

And they were all specialists in something.
All specialists in something, none with a home of his own.

And so now it's a . . .
Has he not got a home neither?

No, he hasn't, he's an Orientalist without a home.
And she's mad about him?

She's madder about him than she's been madder about
    any man.
And you tell me that he's an Orientalist?

That's what I tell you – he's an Orientalist.
You don't tell me!

I do tell you!
The Orientalist. She! The Orientalist.

Doris Fashions

to Sarah

On the instructions of the parole officer, I telephoned the
    prison
At 1 p.m. from the main post office in town.
They said they'd send a prison van in to collect me.
While I was waiting – I had to wait about an hour –
Leaning up against the post-office wall in the noonday sun
I caught a glimpse of myself in the display window
Of a shop across the street – Doris Fashions.
I glimpsed a strange man whom I do not know
And whom when on the odd occasion I have glimpsed him
    before
I have not warmed to – his over-intense visage,
Hurted, hurtful,
All that ice, and all that eyebrow.
I averted my eyes from the mirror-image in Doris Fashions,
Yet thinking that it is good that Doris Fashions –
That there is that much
To be salvaged from the wreckage of the moment –
That Doris Fashions.

If you had a daughter called Doris, and after you had spent
    years
Rearing her and schooling her and enjoying her and loving
    her,
She left home and set up shop in a country town
And called it Doris Fashions – how would you feel?
You would be proud of her, wouldn't you?
Or if you fell in love with a girl called Doris
And it turned out that she had a little shop of her own
Called Doris Fashions – you'd be tickled pink, wouldn't you?

All my life I've dreamed of having a motto of my own –

51

My own logo – my own signature tune.
Waiting for the prison van to collect me,
In the window of Doris Fashions I see through myself
And adopt as my logo, my signature tune,
Doris Fashions –
Trying it out to myself on the road out to the prison:
Doris Fashions Paul Durcan – Paul Durcan Doris Fashions.
For who made the world?
Doris made the world –
And I believe in Doris, and in Doris only,
And never – never – never – never – never – never – never
In John O'Donoghue.

PART
III

The Beckett at the Gate

to Derek Mahon

That spring in Dublin
You could not go anywhere
Without people barking at you,
Buttonholing you in the street and barking at you,
Accosting you and barking at you:
'Have you not seen Barry McGovern's Beckett?'
Or else, which was worse,
'Have you not been to the Beckett at the Gate?'
I was fed up with people barking at me:
'Have you not seen Barry McGovern's Beckett?
Have you not been to the Beckett at the Gate?'

'No, I have not seen Barry McGovern's Beckett –
No, I have not been to the Beckett at the Gate' –
I'd mutter, affecting
To look under my legs
As if it was I
Who was the weary, put-upon virtuoso of bathos,
My limp tail of ejection.
In any case, I am not mad
About going to the theatre –
Going alone to the theatre
Upon a gloomy night in May.
It was, therefore, in spite of myself,
Quite against the grain,
That I took the initiative
By booking a ticket
For a Tuesday night at the Gate
In the third week of May
For Barry McGovern's Beckett,
The Beckett at the Gate.
C9 was the number of my ticket,

Centre, third row from the front.
I got there in good time.
I like to get to a thing in good time
Whatever it is – the bus into town,
Or the bus back out of town –
With at least a quarter of an hour to spare,
Preferably half an hour, ample time
In which to work up an adequate steam of anxiety.
When I stepped into the auditorium
I was relieved to see it was near empty,
I was heartened to see
That it was near empty,
Four or five patrons
Scattered about the theatre.

Consoled, a little less disconcerted
By the general regatta,
A little less addled
By the whole regrettable adventure,
A little less regretful
That I had not stayed put
In my bed-sit,
I made my way to my seat,
Only to discover that one
Of the four or five patrons
Scattered about the near-empty theatre
Transpired to be ensconced
In the adjacent tip-up seat
Right next to my own.
In silence we sat, side by side,
All the house-lights on,
For the entire fifteen minutes before curtain-up.
I felt a right, roaring idiot,
Crouched there in all that silence
In row C of the Gate
Shoulder to shoulder with that –

That other human being –
A woman to boot,
A young woman to boot.

To make matters worse
She was more sprawled than seated,
More dispersed than disposed,
More horizontal than vertical,
Engrossed in a paperback book
The name of which by dint
Of craning of the neck
I did manage to pick out.
It was a Picador paperback
Entitled *One Hundred Years of Solitude*.
As if that was not bad enough
There was not enough leg-room;
So that I had to scrunch up my legs,
Thereby having to sit closer to her.
A minute before the performance began
Someone – obviously some kind of friend,
Some ilk of accomplice –
Hailed her from five rows back:
'Michelle, Michelle!'
I said to myself
If only Michelle's friends
Would invite Michelle to sit with them
Then I'd have all of row C
To myself which at least
Would make the next hour and a half
If not less of a cauchemar
At least a bearable cauchemar.
But no – Michelle stayed put
And the lights went out,
And the curtain up,
And I knew I was for it.
Why had I let myself

Be bothered and browbeaten
By all those cultural groupies
Going on, and on, and on,
'Have you not seen Barry McGovern's Beckett?
Have you not been to the Beckett at the Gate?'

Well, it was out of the top drawer,
As Joseph Holloway would have put it,
Or would not have put it.
Not since the Depression of the 1950s
And the clowns in Duffy's Circus
Have I laughed myself so sorry,
So sorry that I was ready to shout,
If anyone else had shouted:
'Stop Beckett! Stop McGovern!'

And Michelle? Well, Michelle –
I mean talk about Susannah,
Or Judith and Holofernes,
Or any or all of those females
In the Old Testament,
Sarah or Rachel or even Eve;
Not to mention the New Testament,
Martha or Mary or Magdalen –
Michelle was – well, Michelle.
Alright, I ought to have said
She was exceptionally petite –
But it's a small point
And to dwell on it
Would take away from her own performance.
She gave herself over to her own laughter
To such an exuberant extent
That she was entirely inside it – within the orbit
Of her own transparent laughter,
All rouge and polythene.
Every time she laughed

She kicked me in the legs,
In the backs of my legs,
Or nudged me in the kneecaps –
Unintentionally, of course.
Abruptly, she sat up in her seat
Tucking her legs in under her bottom –
Crimson red booties, blue skintight jeans,
Airy black blouse.
She leaned her head on my shoulder,
As if we had been espoused for years,
Donkeys' years, camels' years, elephants' years.
Occasionally, at a particularly
Outrageous piece of malarkey
By Beckett-McGovern,
She'd grip my arm tight
And howl – luminously howl.
Well, obviously, things
Had got quite out of hand
And I wanted to say to her
'Please please please please
Go on doing what you're doing.'
But I did not say anything.
A mum's-the-word man
Is what I am;
Not a word to the Reverend Mother,
Not a smoke-signal to Chief Sitting Mountain.
If there was an interval – and it said
In the programme that there was
An interval of fifteen minutes –
I do not remember any interval.
All I remember is Michelle's head
On my shoulder, and the kick
Of her hair brushing against my cheekbone.
Many years had elapsed since last
I had been made aware of my cheekbone –
Her mousy hair brushing against it,

Scented, and wet, and calamitous.

When the curtain came down
And the applause had drained away
I turned around to gaze
In rapture at Michelle
But she had slipped away.
Mother of God
Chosen by the Eternal Council!
I walked back down along O'Connell Street,
Muttering to myself, repetitiously,
'Have you not seen Barry McGovern's Beckett?
Have you not been to the Beckett at the Gate?'
Every few steps, covertly,
I gave a kick in the air:
'Have you not seen Barry McGovern's Beckett?
Have you not been to the Beckett at the Gate?'
It was dusk – lucid,
Warm, limpid,
On O'Connell Street Bridge.
Spilling over with self-pity
And lasciviously gazing down
At the bicycle-filled waters
Of the River Liffey running on, on,
I elected to walk on
Back to my bed-sit in Ringsend
(Instead of taking the bus)
Through the east European parts of Dublin city,
Past the gasometer and Grand Canal Dock,
Misery Hill, The Gut, The Drain,
The Three Locks – Camden, Buckingham, Westmoreland.
At Ringsend there was a full moon over
The Sugar Loaf and the Wicklow Hills,
And the crimson lights of the telecommunications aerial
On the Three Rock Mountain were trembling
And on the television transmitter in Donnybrook;

And the hand-painted signs of the local public houses,
FitzHarris's and The Oarsman,
Looked childmade in the lamplight, homely
By the River Dodder
As I balanced in a trance on the humpbacked bridge,
On a fulcrum of poignancy,
And I felt like a stranger in a new city,
An urchin in a New Jerusalem,
A bareheaded protagonist
In a vision of reality,
All caught up in a huge romance,
In a hot erotic cold tumult.
On the street corner in Ringsend village
Not at, but close to, a bus-stop,
A tiny young woman was standing,
Hovering, twirling, stamping,
And when I saw that it was Michelle –
As I passed her by
She scrutinised me serenely
As if she had never seen me before –
As if she had never seen me before.
I keep on walking;
I'll go on, I think, I'll go on.
Next year in Carrickmines
I'll play tennis with whatever
Woman will play tennis with me
And I'll never be never again.
Next year in Carrickmines.
On grass. Love all.
Fifteen Love. Thirty Love. Forty Love.
Deuce. Advantage Miss Always.
Game, Set and Match.
Why you, Michelle, why you –
Will you join me? Join me?
If you're the joining kind, please join me.
Next year in Carrickmines,

Greystones, Delgany, Killiney, Bray, Dalkey, Shankill, Kilmacud,
Galloping Green, Stillorgan – perhaps even Dublin.

There's a beckett at the gate, there's a beckett
at the gate, Michelle;
There's a Beckett at the gate, there's a Beckett
at the gate, Michelle;
There's a beckett at the Gate, there's a beckett
at the Gate, Michelle;
There's a Beckett at the Gate, there's a Beckett
at the Gate, Michelle.

PART
IV

Going Home to Russia

to A. Voznesensky

Hanging about the duty-free in Shannon Airport,
Waiting for the flight to Moscow to be called;
Waiting for the Havana–Moscow Illushin 62
To come in for refuelling, and to pick me up.

I am the solitary passenger joining the flight at Shannon;
The Irish immigration officer eyes me mournfully;
'Good luck,' he mutters as if to say 'you will need it';
He does not know that I am versed in luck.

'Good luck,' he mutters as if to a hostage or convict,
Not knowing that he is speaking to an Irish dissident
Who knows that in Ireland scarcely anybody is free
To work or to have a home or to read or write.

We Irish have had our bellyful of *blat*
And *blarney*, more than our share
Of the *nomenklatura* of Church and Party,
The *nachalstvo* of the legal and medical mafia.

Going down the airbridge, I slow my step,
Savouring the moment of liberation;
As soon as I step aboard the Aeroflot airliner
I will have stepped from godlessness into faith:

Into a winter of shoe-swapping;
Into a springtime of prams;
Into a summer of riverbanks and mountain huts;
Into an autumn of mushroom-hunting.

It is not until I am aboard the carrier
That I realise I am going home;

I have been ill at ease – on tenterhooks –
Because I have not realised I am going home.

Yet the doorway of the aircraft is still open;
The airbridge has not yet been disconnected;
At the last moment I might be taken off –
Not until we are airborne will I be free.

At the entrance to the cabin the pilot looms,
Shirt-sleeves rolled up to his elbows;
He has the look of the long-distance bus driver
On the Galway–Limerick–Cork route:

A man much loved by his wife and friends;
The shape of his mind is the shape of the route;
Smoking his Cosmos, what is he thinking of?
He knows every bend in the road, every skyline,

And that the world, despite obstinate man, is round.
He will bend over the Baltic;
He will turn a corner at Riga, and at Moscow
He will let Asia run her fingers through our hair.

Take-off – the hips of the Shannon Estuary;
The pores of the gooseflesh of Ireland;
Wet, unrequited yearnings by the prickly inch;
The River Shannon lying crumpled on the mudflats of
    Foynes.

Goodbye to the conscientious politicians of Ireland
Who believe in the Right of the Few to Free Speech
But not in the Right of the Many to Work and Health,
Housing, Transport, Education, Art.

Goodbye to the penniless, homeless, trouserless politicians;
Goodbye to the pastoral liberals and the chic gombeens;

Goodbye to the gobberloos and the looderamauns;
Goodbye to the wide boys and their wider wives.

Goodbye to the squires and the squiresses
And their clerical leg-men in the bishops' palaces
Whose function it is to keep the masses in their places.
A mitre who fails to keep a pig in its poke

Will get the message pronto on the golf club telephone:
'Bishop Comfy – Central Committee of Commerce here –
Your pups in the pulpits must poke the pigs –
The last thing we want is freedom for the people.'

Copenhagen – the Baltic – Riga – Smolensk –
If there be a heaven, then this is what
It must feel like to be going down into heaven –
To be going home to Russia.

Beyond Smolensk the long approach begins,
The long approach into Moscow;
From far out at an angle of forty-five degrees,
The long descent into Sheremetyeva.

By his engine-murmurs, the pilot sounds like a man
Who has chosen to make love instead of to rape;
He caresses the Russian plains
With a long, slow descent – a prolonged kiss

With the night down below us, with Russia
Under her mantle of snow and forest;
A block of flats lights up out of nowhere –
The shock in a lover's eyes at the impact of ecstasy.

O Svetka, Svetka! Don't, don't!
Say my name, O say my name!
O God O Russia! Don't, don't!

Say my name, O say my name!

In the aftermath of touchdown, gently we taxi;
We do not immediately put on our clothes;
In the jubilation of silence we taste our arrival –
The survival of sex.

The nose of the jet interlocks with the doorway;
At the top of the airbridge a militiaman stands smiling;
Outside the arrivals building I get lost in the snow;
I meet a woman who is also lost in the snow.

Going home to Russia to be with you –
Dark secret of life;
Going home to Russia to be with you –
Svetka in the snow.

Block after block after block after block –
You are squeaky-sick with laughter that I've come home;
Your neighbour, Madame Noses, sneaks a peep at me –
Dear, dear Svetka.

For sure I have no tv, and my radio
I use only for these weather reports:
This way we do it – it is good, no?
There are so many of us, so many.

I have come home to you to greet you –
To watch with you the trains for Yaroslavl;
Train after train from the fifth-storey window –
What contentment! It is Moscow, and we are alone.

I have come home to you to greet you
In your own tiny kitchen – a kitchen lit for lovers;
To press red maple leaves between the pages of books,
To take off my tin hat and put on your shoes;

To sleep with you on the settee and to become with you
Creatures of the forest, crushed deer;
Never again to have to endure the persecution
Of landlords, the humiliation of advertisers;

To live again with nature as before I lived
In Ireland before all the trees were cut down;
Again collecting leaves in Moscow in October,
Closer to you than I am to myself.

My dear loved one, let me lick your nose;
Nine months in your belly, I can smell your soul;
Your two heads are smiling – not one but both of them –
Isn't it good, Svetka, good, that I have come home?

O Svetka, Svetka! Don't, don't!
Say my name, O say my name!
O God O Russia! Don't, don't!
Say my name, O say my name.

The Red Arrow

In the history of transport – is there any other history? –
The highest form of transport is the Red Arrow,
The night train from Leningrad to Moscow.
With whom will I be sharing my compartment tonight?
The editor of the *Jazz Front Gazette*, it transpires.
But, affable, polite, as she is, how can she compare
With Svetka with whom I shared in 1981?
We sat up half the night chinwagging, colloguing,
And when awkwardly I began to undress and she said:
'Ah yes, it is alright – would you like to?'
Naturally I liked to,
And the train was about half way between Leningrad and
   Moscow
When I fell out of my bunk on to the floor
And the wagon-lady put her head in the door
To check what was the matter
And Svetka said in Russian: 'These foreigners –
They cannot even keep from falling out of bed –
Always needing to be treated like babies.'
The wagon-lady grunted and slid the door shut
And I climbed back into the bunk with Svetka.
Each time we made love she groaned:
'I am the little horse in your snow'
And I let up the blinds and, as we made love again –
A blizzard upside down at the windowpane –
Each time she opened her eyes, she murmured
'You are snowing on my tail, my dear man.'
As the Red Arrow shot into Moscow, Svetka said:
'My dear man, you must meet me tomorrow.
Tell them you have a problem with your business.
Meet me in the Melodiya Music Store on Kalinin.
I will be in the Classical Russian Music section.
Look me up under Rachmaninov.'

It was a grey Moscow afternoon – not a bead of sunlight –
But we traipsed up and down the Arbat in seventh heaven.
'My dear, dear man,' she keeps murmuring over and over
Although that was all of seven years ago –
She who shot the Red Arrow through my heart.

The Puppet Theatre in Akopyan Street

to G. S. Igitian

Back in Dublin and New York and London,
In Paris and Berlin and Amsterdam,
Cultural folk like to preach at brunch about freedom.
Freedom – they prunch – is what you have in the West.
Freedom – they prunch – is what you do not have in Russia.
Yet tonight, on a vicious winter's night,
In the attic of the Puppet Theatre in Akopyan Street
I am as free as I will ever be.

True, the puppeteers back home are free:
But it is a question of degree.
In the art of manipulation
– Or should we call it conduct, the art of the ethical? –
Here in the attic of the Puppet Theatre in Akopyan Street
I am free to be the child I yearn to be.
The big, gay man and the small, grave girl plead with me
To be what I am, and in the sleet-flak of their pleas
I begin to move my lips in harmony with my hands,
And forms of conversation become forms of love-making.

But the big man does not accuse me of perversity
As I rear up behind him gazing down his spine;
And in the grave girl's eyes I am not a rapist
Although she is trapped in a corner as I advance on her,
Each hand an open-mouthèd knife and my knees swaying.
'Why don't you write a poem about *Glasnost*?' she asks
And – in the silence of my reply – 'Why don't you
Come home with us tonight to our flat in Kirovskaya?'

Downstairs on the sidewalk there are apparatchiks in blue
　　jeans
Smoking Marlborough and drinking Pepsi through straws,

72

Conspiring to open a McDonald's Hamburger Restaurant in
  Gorki.
They want to clench me at every turn of the screw;
The Puppet Theatre in Akopyan Street is anathema to them.
But what can they do? I am a go-lucky marionette,
A trueborn snob, a man of the people,
Knowing that nobody can perceive my strings.
I don't smoke and I drink only Armenian cognac.
Nobody can perceive me praying to Lenin.
Have mercy on me! Power to the children.

Bringing Home the Water-Melon from Samarkand

to E. Shepilova

I loved Papa – even though he was an old bollox.
But my patience – and Mama's patience –
Ran out the day he made a hames
Of bringing home the water-melon from Samarkand.

All he had to do was to carry them back on the plane,
Carry them back in his arms on the plane,
A pair of enormous, oval, tubular, golden
Water-melon from Samarkand,
Each of them tied up erotically in a string bag –
Metaphysical brassières, perchance, Andrushka –
But he was embarrassed – he complained – embarrassed,
Holding in his arms a pair of melons.
It made him look – he shushshushed – like a woman with
    bosoms.
Askance my mother glared at him across the tip-up table
At 29,000 feet over the Caspian Sea,
Trembling her own great pair of bosoms at him:
She swore silently – 'These are mine, my melons.'

But Papa combined to act the dog in the manger
And the hurt, injured, sad son of a bitch
At 29,000 feet over the Caspian Sea.
To evade the issue, he barked at me
What he has been barking at me for forty-two years:
'The Caspian – Sturgeon's Roe – Caviar – Beluga – *Huso
    huso!*'
Mama leaned across and took hold of one melon
And planted it between her buoyant, floating bosoms,
Resting her double chin in the cup of her hand,
Gazing out of a porthole from her seat on the outside aisle,
Thinly smiling to herself.

Men are not capable even of being women
And the burden of life goes on,
Goes on being a woman's burden, burden,
Bringing home the water-melon from Samarkand.

The Return of Solzhenitsyn

Alexander Isayevich, for how much longer
Will we have to wait for you to come home?
It has been twelve years now since last you clapped
Your mittens in Gorki Street and marvelled at the fumes
Of your own breath writhing in the Russian air.
For twelve years now we have waited –
Don't you think it is time for you to think of us
Who require and implore you to come home?
Prodigal son whom we revere and cherish,
Not least a party man such as myself
Who was only an apparatchik of twenty-two
When Queen Brezhnev kicked you out.
Alexander Isayevich, we have served our sentence:
Have mercy on us and, if you please, come home.

Peredelkino: at the Grave of Pasternak

to A. K. Avelichev

I

After all these years, Boris Leonidovich Pasternak,
I have found you.
How self-engrossed and paranoid I must appear to you
Lurking at the foot of your grave,

A blue corduroy cap on my head
That I purchased in a West of Ireland village;
A green scarf tied around my throat,
A Japanese automatic camera in my hand.

But you are not vexed by my foibles –
If anything you rejoice in and applaud me –
A middle-aged gear-laden telephone engineer
Frantic to grapple with your trinity of pines.

Be still, my strapped-up and harnessed soul.
I begin at last to stand at ease.
Instead of grappling with them, I overhear myself
Conversing with the Father, the Son and the Holy Spirit.

But it is they who do most of the conversing.
I am amazed by their point of view.
Although the enemy once again is almost
At the gates of Moscow and Borodino

They egg me to pay no heed:
Instead of darkening my energy
With bombast and humbug
I should paint my soul with leaves of mud.

While warplanes fly to and fro overhead
And cars race up and down the Kiev Highway,
Pay heed to the housewife on the skyline,
On whose head God has put a price.

At the heart of atheism God is at home;
Man locked into history opening the door.
Closer to God is the atheist opening the door
Than the churchman closing the door in your face.

II

Strange that anybody can visit your grave,
    Even a naïf like me;
Surely the dead are entitled to privacy,
    If not also the living.

Your grave out here in the Vineyard of Peredelkino
    Is open to all comers:
I gaze through the railings at your headstone,
    Let myself in by the gate.

I am borne back to another railing'd grave
    In Kilcrea in West Cork:
'Lo Arthur Leary, generous, handsome, brave,
    Slain in his bloom lies in this humble grave.'

Slain in his bloom like you,
    Lo Boris Leonidovich;
Who died for the right to ride a white horse;
    You – generous, handsome, brave.

Sitting down on the wooden bench, I note
    That it is I who am trapped in life
Whilst in death you are free,
    Golden eagle on a black leaf.

Over the grave of Art O'Leary at midnight
    On a summer's evening,
Your young priestlike friend from Zima, Yevtushenko,
    Broke – broke a bottle of red wine.

Somewhere in the petals of the crowd in the metro
    My lost mother is peering out at me;
My mother who went to Russia when I was three
    And who stayed in Moscow.

Somewhere in the trees of the hand-painted forest
    Ivinskaya is peering out at me;
A man without his woman is a right hand without a left;
    I kiss the back of her hand.

Voices of a man and a woman through the foliage,
    A father and mother
At the fresh grave next to yours of a nineteen-year-old boy
    Slain in the Afghanistan wars.

I have not read the novel of Dr Zhivago,
    Yet I lack the courage to say so;
Isn't it heartbreakingly funny how relentlessly
    Pretentious men are.

How often I myself have met intellectuals
    Who have read Bulgakov
They say – whose faces go blank if you talk
    To them about Titian Tabidze.

All alone at your grave, I have a two-hour conversation
    With myself and the trees;
My blue corduroy cap perched all alone
    On the damp bench watching us.

A babushka is propelling herself like a pram

Across the road with three goats;
In the car returning to Moscow, the driver remarks
    'Your blue cap looks Jewish – is it German?'

That night we make love in an apartment beside
    The Cultural Palace of the Ball-Bearing Plant;
Next morning under Shevchenko's statue by the
    Moskva River
        I set fire to my cap.

O Song of the Blue Cap, for Boris Leonidovich,
    From the West of Ireland.
It makes a soft explosion (two books of matches inside it),
    An orgasm of gentleness.

In the leaf-strewn post-coital smoke-pall
    The cars do not stop reiterating your name
As they race down Kalinin Prospekt to Red Square –
    Pasternak! Pasternak!

Moskviches, Zhigulis, Volgas, Chaikas,
    And the odd, conspicuous Zill:
Pasternak, Pasternak! Pasternak, Pasternak!
    Victory to the Blue Cap Boy.

Trauma Junction

The answer to your question is that I am not your mother;
Your mother was another mother and she died in Russia.

Estonian Farewell

to Arvo

Midwinter in the snowed-up port of Tallinn,
Midnight on the platform of Tallinn railway station,
Leaning out the window of the midnight train
As it begins to pull out for Leningrad and fever,
And Arvo rooted to the platform waving farewell to us,
Clutching in his hands
A little book in blue-and-gold wrappers –
Teach Yourself Irish by Myles Dillon.

Arvo, I have been to the moon and found you;
I wave and you wave; you wave and I wave;
As you squat there in your furry nimbus,
And my mother – a ghost with a knife through her halo –
Is stumbling through the trees to keep up with the train,
The trees between the tracks and the fields,
And she is crying, crying, crying, crying,
'My son, my son, why hast thou forsaken me?'

The Kindergarten Archipelago

And as wet dusk filters into a remote Russian town
I am aware of being watched as I scurry
Down Marx Prospekt towards my room – watched
By a schoolgirl with a hamster in her hand.
Suddenly as I sway there, standing
With an umbrella spilling black ink above my head,
I see that what is strange about the Soviet Union
Is that it cherishes all the children of the union equally.
Surely a fellow needs help who does not see that nothing
Is of consequence except the children of the union.
And so, while Alexander Solzhenitsyn tramps the marches
Of his walled-off home-in-exile in Vermont, USA,
Under the flying black skies of Ryazan
I am sailing the streets of the Kindergarten Archipelago.

Zina in Murmansk

As a schoolgirl, Zina
Was all that a Pioneer instructor
Could dream of, and her parents –
Druzhniki, gribniki,
Peace-keepers, mushroom-hunters –
Were proud of her as a mushroom,
Their own miniscule red mushroom.
She was droll, elegant, gay,
Her company always a pleasure.
It was expected that after schooldays
She would attend the Literary Institute
In Moscow, or the Leningrad Art College.
Instead, she became a grade-A typist
And applied for a resident's permit
In Murmansk, in the arctic region
Of the Far North.
Zina – diminutive of Zinaida –
Had always been a dreamer
With her feet on the ground.
She was certain that Murmansk
Was the kind of town she would find
The old-fashioned man she yearned for,
A specimen of manhood whose ancestors
Had been living the same sort of life
For thousands and thousands and thousands of –
A Mesolithic Man of the twentieth century
Who would fish for shark in the White Sea
And hunt polar bear in the tundra,
Who would live with her in a log cabin
And at night read to her from Tolstoy,
Valentin Rasputin and Chingitz Aitmatov,
While she darned his mighty socks,
Or applied her awl to his boots,
Boring tunnels for thong piping.

But such men are no more extant
In Murmansk than in Moscow.
She could not find even one man
Who had a drop of Mesolithic sexuality
Left in his pasteurised blood.
To this day Zina remains
A single girl in Murmansk,
Typing out the correspondence of the chairman
Of the White Sea Shipping Company,
At 18 Komintern Street,
While he attends to his fourth wife
And the nightly routine of television and fornication.
It is the same the wide world over
From Murmansk to Batumi,
From Novosibirsk to Shamaka:
A question of whether or not there is *time*
– Time, I said, time, time and time again –
To squeeze in a quick fornication
Between the 9 p.m. newscast
And the 9.30 p.m. current affairs, musical chairs programme.
Soon shark and bear will be extinct –
And women too:
Soon there will be no more women.
Zina goes nightly to her bunk
As to her belovèd grave.
Reading in bed late at night in Murmansk,
Am I the last woman left alive in the world?

Tbilisi Cabaret (Ortachala Belle with a Fan)

in memoriam *N. Pirosmani*

I'm a sophisticated primitive.
I'm going bald but I don't chase
After my hair, and when I sway
My hips – it's for you.
Tell me you appreciate my authoritative wrists,
Tell me you savour the scent of my sweat,
And I will tell you on your fortieth birthday
That you're a girl at heart.

O my dear one, warm to me.
I will always warm to you.

I'm a sophisticated primitive.
It is you who is the prima donna
Forever much more prima and more donna
Than the man who likes to state –
The man who is not afraid to state –
That love is greater than God or Marx.
A woman's love made the world.
I believe in woman.

O my dear one, warm to me.
I will always warm to you.

I'm a sophisticated primitive.
I like to bring my own chair
To the party, and at the height
Of the party there is nowhere I like better
To sit than under the table nursing
A bottle of you, your smiling silence,
Until abruptly, after sixty-nine years,
You winkle me out and lick me.

O my dear one, warm to me.
I will always warm to you.

I am a citizen of a secret society.
Although God was born in Russia
It is a well-kept secret.
In Red Square on Palm Sunday
I looked through Brezhnev's eyes
When they were open, and I saw
Ten thousand secrets wave up at me.
'Jesus, it's May Day!' he said to me.

O my dear one, warm to me.
I will always warm to you.

Our Lady of Red Square, pray for us.
Midnight Trolleybus, pray for us.
Icecream in Winter, pray for us.
Queen of the Moscow Metro, pray for us.
Leaf of Gold, pray for us.
Hammer and Sickle, pray for us.
Mother of Intercourse, pray for us.
Taxi at Dawn, pray for us.

Ortachala Belle, may to me on May Day.
On May Day may I always may to you.

The Woman with the Keys to Stalin's House

You would imagine – would you not –
That the town of Gori,
The town of Joseph Vissarionovich Dzhugashvili,
By virtue of being just that –
Stalin's home town –
Would be a self-centred, uninhabited, pock-marked crater,
'The town that gave birth to . . .'

But I had the luck to meet Galina
– Galya –
Who has lived all her life in the town of Gori
Under the statue of Stalin,
A buxom, humorous, lugubrious woman,
Her ashblonde nail-varnish matching her ashblonde hair
Corbelled in a pony-tail.
After traipsing about the Stalin Museum
And the house where Stalin was born,
Which Stalin personally had preserved as a monument to
    himself –
Sentimental Soso –
We had a meal together in the local hotel
Around the corner in Stalin Square.
'I am the saddest woman in all Georgia,'
She remarked to me with a smile
That played on her mauve-painted lips
Long after her words had died,
Spreadeagling her arms
So that her breasts could breathe
In the suffocating atmosphere,
Black rain knifing the windowpane.
While we ate and drank in silence
She opened the buttons of her blouse,
Beckoning me to follow suit.
She motioned to me to open my mouth

And swilling her own mouth with champagne,
She put her lips to mine,
Letting the champagne swill
Into my mouth from her mouth.
The mountains askew above the town
Leaned slightly across the sky
As we lurched around the room
Making big love and little love.
Afterwards we bathed one another
With a jug and a basin;
As I towelled her down
She shut her eyes, tightly.
Stalin Street was deserted
As we embraced goodbye,
Imagining that we would never meet again.
She remarked:
'I like you a little because you have mixed feelings.'
In the car returning to Tbilisi,
Riding down the Georgian Military Highway,
I considered that if Eve had been even half-as-affectionate
As Galina in Gori,
Well, how lucky I was to have been her Adam;
And Jahweh – that old Stalin on his plinth –
Had failed to cow us. Galya,
Can there be anyone in the world who has not got mixed
    feelings?
Should there be anyone in the world who has not got mixed
    feelings?

The Fairy Tale of 1937

in memoriam *A. Tarkovsky*

Once upon a time there a czar called S
Who was afeard of a wanderer called M
Because M, who was a stubble-faced and wispy fellow
With thick red lips and soft white teeth,
Had the peculiar habit of what we call
'Giving ourselves back to ourselves' –
Like Bulat Okudzhava, in our own era.
That is to say, whenever M met you on the golden boulevard,
And you were not in the best of sorts, even out of sorts,
He'd kiss you on both cheeks and put his arms around you,
All very quietly, undemonstratively, and he'd say –
Like Bruce Springsteen –
With a quick burst of a laugh, with but a quick burst of a
    laugh –
'Jesus, let me give you back to yourself.'
He'd look you straight in the face –
His blue, granny eyes grinning out at you.

The Czar S became so afeard of M
That he issued a ukase
That every telephone in Russia was to be shot dead.
By the end of 1936 every telephone in Russia and Georgia
Had been shot dead.
But still M was wandering about Moscow and Leningrad and
    Tbilisi
Giving people back to themselves . . .
So that in 1937 the Czar S had M interned
And committed to an empty psychiatric hospital
In a derelict cul-de-sac on the docks,
Sentencing him to total and solitary confinement forever.
To this day nobody has ever set foot in that house
And it is known to us all as House 1937:

Operator, please get me One-Nine-Three-Seven . . .

One day someone – a red woman
Will step through a wall into the House of 1937
And what will she find there?
On his back wandering in the rain?
Sitting in the chair by the window?
With his feet in a milkpail of rainwater?
Stretched out on the iron bed in the corner?
With his head on a bolster of rainwater?
She will find one-and-a-half million people
Pressed between the pages of poetry books,
Not even their tongues or their toes curled up at the edges,
Not even their clitorises or penises curled up at the edges,
Not even the serrated peripheries of their brains curled up at
    the edges.

O my Red Jesus,
Let me be the harlot who will step back into 1937,
The House on the Docks,
To heap up my elbows around your smiling knees,
And to kiss-with-my-tongue, kiss-with-my-tongue,
    kiss-with-my-tongue
Your big-eared, wide-eyed feet.

The Prodigal Son

(after Rembrandt)

to A. Cronin

I can see them crawling on all fours towards me –
My father and mother across the Armenian carpet,
Coaxing, cajoling, conniving, conspiring,
Fangs of the coal fire among their earlobes and eyelashes:
'Watch out for the Bogey Man at the bottom of the back
    garden,
The Bogey Man in the coal pit at the bottom of the back
    garden.
He is coming to eat you – he has the biggest tummy in Russia.
He has spikes where his hands should be
And his ruby lips are smeared with refined white sugar.'

From the frail safety net of the windowpane
I stare out aghast at the silhouette of the coal pit,
Waiting for the Bogey Man to make the first move,
To uncrumple himself and come swaying into the window,
To affix his spikes to my shoulderblades, his pot-belly to my
    skull,
His lips to my lips and to snuff out my life.
What must it be like to be a Bogey Man?
What are the practical difficulties of being a Bogey Man?
The domestic logistics of inhabiting a coal pit?
What must he look like?
I can envisage his arms and his torso but not his face –
Except for his ruby lips smeared with refined white sugar.

But when he was yet a great way off, his father saw him,
And had compassion, and ran, and fell on his neck, and
    kissed him.

Tonight, past midnight, thirty-five years later
As I crouch on the edge of my bed
In my third-floor waterfront room in the Hotel Leningrad,
Too scared to switch on a light,
I see that all my life I have been waiting
For the Bogey Man at the bottom of the back garden.
Twenty minutes ago, when on a deserted street off the
    Nevsky Prospekt,
At the junction of three humpbacked canal bridges
Caught up in one solitary street lamp,
A small old man in fur and felt
Stepped out of the lurking shadows
With a pitchfork in his hand
And shouted to me
– With a jovial air –
'How are you there!'
I recoiled – wanting only to bury my head
In the pit of his bosom,
Wanting only to receive
His blotched, ravaged hands on my young thighs
And his tiny voice booming:
Welcome home, son, welcome home.
All is forgiven, son, all is forgiven.

Diarrhoea Attack at Party Headquarters in Leningrad

An attack of diarrhoea at Party Headquarters in Leningrad
Was not something I imagined ever happening to me –
Which is perhaps partly why it did happen to me.
The presidium had barely taken its place
Under the iconic portraits of V.I. Lenin and M.S. Gorbachev
When I could feel the initial missiles
Firing down the sky of my stomach
Setting in motion something that was irreversible –
The *realpolitik* of the irreversible.
The only consolation was that I was wearing underpants.
The fact is that sometimes I do not wear underpants.
Oddly enough I was wearing red underpants
Which I had originally purchased in Marks & Spencers.
The first explosion resulted in immediate devastation –
The ensuing explosions serving only to define
The innately irreversible dialectic of catastrophe.
I whispered magnanimously into the earhole of my
    interpreter.
He reciprocated that since he also had 'a trauma of the
    intestine'
We should both take our leave *immédiatement* and he
    showed me
Such fraternal solicitude that in my mind's eye
I can still see Lenin peering down at me
As if he were peering at nobody else in the hall.
A black Volga whisked us back to our hotel and ignominy –
My ignominy – not anybody else's ignominy – and that night
Over cups of tea we discussed the war in Afghanistan,
Agreeing that realistically it appeared an insoluble problem,
Yet hoping against hope that somehow it would be solved
And that – as you put it, Slava – 'Russian boys come home'.
There is nothing necessarily ignominious about anything.

94

Hymn to my Father

Dear Daddy on your last legs now,
Can you hear me
In your bedroom in the treetops,
In your top-storey sarcophagus,
Chained to your footwarmer and your pills,
Death notices in newspapers your exclusive reading?
We had no life together – or almost none.
Yet you made me what I am –
A man in search of his Russia.
After schooldays I became a poet –
A metamorphosis you could no more fathom
Than I could fathom your own osmosis –
Lawyer with a secret life,
As secret as the life of a poet.
You had a history for every milestone,
A saga for every placename
– The Bovril Sign, the Ballast Office Clock, the Broadstone –
And so, at your knee, at your elbow, I became you.
Estranged as we are,
I am glad that it was in this life
I loved you,
Not the next.
O Russian Knight at the Crossroads!
If you turn to the right, you will lose your horse;
To the left, your head;
If you go straight on, your life.
If you were me – which you are –
Knight at the Crossroads,
You would go home to Russia this very night.

Red Square – the Hours

'Religious suffering is at once the expression of real suffering and the protest against real suffering. Religion is the sigh of the oppressed creature, the heart of a heartless world, just as it is the spirit of spiritless conditions.' – Karl Marx

At some stage God must have been alive
In St Peter's Square
But she is certainly not alive there now –
Poor murdered woman.

God lives in Red Square.
It is the first thing that strikes you
On a February morning
Standing on the corner of October The Twenty-Fifth Street

And Red Square;
And that the world is round
And that, at the heart of the heartless world, God –
She is not dead.

The silence of Red Square at noon –
Cobblestones and skylines;
Militiamen beside me munching icecreams,
Women with little microphones selling lottery tickets,

Married couples photographing one another under fir trees,
Mud-bespattered youths with shovels on their shoulders,
And across the square under the Kremlin wall
The queue closing and unclosing its eyelids:

Flicking its tail, stamping its feet,
Theologians at its head, children in its tummy,
Flexing its muscles, licking its fur,
The business of business is not business.

The people are yearning to pray
At the tomb of the Son of Man;
At the heart of the heartless world
Pilgrims from Uzbekistan

And Siberia at the tomb of Lenin.
Near the Spassky Gate
An old lady in a Ukrainian headscarf
Shakes hands across a crush barrier

With a boy militiaman.
Another old lady is chatting up the driver
Of a big black Chaika.
At the heart of the heartless world

She chuckles that when she says what she thinks
She means something else –
That the people
Should all have big black Chaikas.

She laughs; he laughs with her.
She asks me affably how I am keeping.
The Spassky Tower chimes on the quarter.
On the hour, the changing of the guard.

The People of Red Square
Have the nerve to look upon the cosmos
As a Primitive Family:
Only an Akhmatova, a Mandelstam

Could, without articles, put into nouns
My peace of mind,
In spite of all the pain,
In Red Square at noon.

Which is not to say that the afternoon

Does not bring with it humdrum terrors:
A phonecall from a party yeti;
A dog's dinner in the canteen.

But I'm lucky – and at midnight
I go walking in Red Square:
In Red Square at midnight in the snow
Courting couples walking to and fro.

Onion domes, red walls,
Cobblestones calling me home.
O heart of the heartless world –
Dear heart, forgive me.

I am not afraid to lose you,
I am not afraid of my fear.
Neither the Kremlin Mountaineer
Nor the White House Cowboy

Can finger either of us now
Among the Beatitudes and the Cobblestones.
At the heart of the heartless world – God:
She is alive in Red Square.

John Field's Dressing-Gown with Onion Domes and Spires

'Take a right turn at the Sputnik Cinema' –
These were the street directions from an abrupt,
Voluptuous passerby, in black high-heel boots
And rabbit-skin fur hat,
On how to find the Vedenskoye Cemetery
In which the nineteenth-century Irish pianist
And composer, John Field, lies buried.

Behind the Sputnik Cinema on the side of a hill
Overlooking the Yauza River
Across the road from the deserted tennis courts
– High wire netting melancholy against the sky –
A pastoral red kremlin I had never seen before:
A long, high, crenellated redbrick wall
And behind it a forest of birch and pine
In among the mausolea and the tombs.

Madame Nina, the caretaker, was reluctant
To guide me to your grave
For fear that as your fellow-countryman
I would be mortified by its delapidated,
Untended condition – I assured Madame Nina
I would not be mortified, and she believed me.
What was aggravating her was that a week had elapsed
Since she had last had time to polish you –
A half-dozen or so mussels of bird-droppings
Adorned your green marble quilt.

As we strolled down the aisles of tombstones and trees
It struck me as curious that while travellers
Correctly pay homage to the cemeteries of Paris
– Père-Lachaise, Montparnasse, Montmartre, Passy –
Nobody sings the praises of the cemeteries of Moscow

– Novodevichy, Vagankovskoye, Pyatnitskoye –
And now, the most stately cemetery in Russia,
The Vedenskoye.

Madame Nina bustled ahead of me,
Five or six paces ahead of me,
Believing, as she remarked afterwards,
That I should be left alone with my own thoughts.
But instead of piety or grief or awe
I felt that apologetic awkwardness
One feels as one tiptoes down the corridors
Of a big city hospital, down the aisles past the beds
To visit one's father whom one has never met,
The legendary, mythical, prodigal father.

You were sitting up in bed, and when you saw me
You stammered 'O my poor – poor boy'
And beckoning to Madame Nina to leave us alone
You grasped my two hands and shook your head.
With my head in your breast, I stared
At your blue-and-gold, silk, fur-trimmed dressing-gown
With onion domes and spires.

The old ladies of the cemetery
Gathered themselves round us
With their brooms and wheelbarrows,
Their shovels and buckets.
Madame Nina proffered me a yellow leaf
Which I placed at the foot of your grave.
It was only twelve o'clock noon,
Yet already the Moscow sky was darkening,
Making goldener the cupolas of golden leaves,
Goldener also the black mud,
Goldener October.
As I steadied myself to take a last photograph
You produced from under your pillow

The italicised inscription on your tomb:

Erected
To His Memory
By
Mis Grateful Friends
and
Scholars
John Field
Born in Ireland
in 1782
Dead in Moscow
in 1837.

After mulling the wine of the idiosyncratic syntax
I hid behind a birch and said last prayers.
You murmured again – no need for such as you to clamour
Or to put your foot down on the pedal –
You murmured:
'I have been living in the Vedenskoye Cemetery
For one hundred and forty-nine years;
That is w'what it m'means to be *Dead in Moscow*.
And to h'have *Mis Grateful Friends in Moscow*
Is to be cherished by women whose nerve and verve
– O the diabolical shoulderblades of women! –
Would put to s'shame all the m'marshals of h'history;
Louise, Maria, Agate – and Ekaterina
Who subscribed one hundred roubles to my erection.'

The photographs came back from the printers
With a tag: *Blank Film*.

Dasvidanya, John Field – Nobody of the Nocturne.
A nobody in Gorki Street,
I wrap myself, against my fate of rain,
In your blue-and-gold, silk, fur-trimmed dressing-gown
With onion domes and spires.

101

John Field Visits his Seventy-Eight-Year-Old
  Widowed Mother

When I went round to see Mother on Sunday night
I found her dead in bed. Dead in bed.
I who am renowned for being 'Dead in Moscow'.
I don't know. I straightened out her pillow.
I tucked in the blankets that had come loose.
I tried to make her more comfortable.
I folded her hands across her breast
Because I thought she looked more – more herself that way.
I don't know. I lit a candle on her bedside table.
I sat down beside her like I always do –
Watching the grease coagulate and coalesce.
I crossed my knees and listened to the silence.
We often do that – Mother and I – listen to the silence:
Not spoiling everything with dialogue.
There is too much dialogue in the world.
Silence is what is wanted. Silence.
I don't know. I stood up and gazed out the window
At my vague, dissipated face, pockmarked with tears.
I sat down at the pianoforte, and played
For Mother dead in bed my Nocturne in E flat major.
It sounded much more textured than before.
The circumstance of Mother's being dead in bed
May have enriched it, I suppose – I don't know.
Her fruit cakes were always rich, all raisins and almonds.
I invented the Nocturne on the basis of her fruit cake:
Retaining the icing – dispensing with the actual cake.
Dead in bed. Mother. Dead in bed.
I who am renowned for being 'Dead in Moscow'.